T0258517

G A L E N

and the Gateway to Medicine

by JEANNE BENDICK

Pictures by the author

Bethlehem Books • Ignatius Press
Bathgate N.D. San Francisco

Text and illustrations © 2002 Jeanne Bendick
Introduction © 2002 Benjamin D. Wiker

Cover art by Jeanne Bendick
Cover design by Davin Carlson

All rights reserved

Third printing, August 2024

ISBN: 978-1-883937-75-1
Library of Congress catalog number: 2002108552

Bethlehem Books • Ignatius Press
10194 Garfield Street South
Bathgate, ND 58216
www.bethlehembooks.com
1-800-757-6831

Printed in the United States on acid-free paper

Contents

To all the doctors who look after us

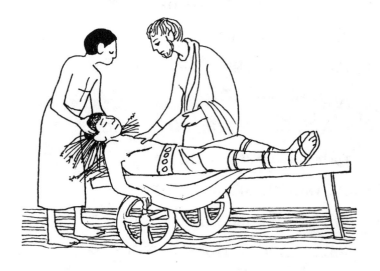

Introduction

Human beings find the truth about things very slowly, with much effort, and with more than an occasional wrong turn. As Aristotle, the great Greek philosopher, rightly said, our minds are to the truth, as the eyes of bats to the sun. In short, progress in knowledge generally follows a rather winding path, guided as much by the educated guesses of the explorers as by the nature of what is being explored.

That having been said, some are better at guessing than others—or to be more exact, some guesses are more educated than others. The men of great genius, whose contributions advance human theoretical and practical knowledge by great leaps rather than little steps, always prepare themselves well by attending carefully to the contributions of those who came before them.

Galen's genius, in great part, lay in his sorting through all the best in medical knowledge that had been handed down by the Greeks, separating the good from the bad, and building upon the good. Born at the height of the Roman Empire, in the second century A.D., Galen pulled medicine from the thickets into which various confusions and controversies had led it, and set it on a straight path again.

If we can judge the genius of Galen insofar as his account of the art of medicine influenced later generations, then Galen was the greatest physician of all time. He corrected Greek medicine, and gave it to the Romans. The roads from Rome carried Galen's works all over the Empire. After the Empire had fallen, and its famous roads were broken and overgrown, Galen's influence only grew, moving through the Byzantine empire and the Arab-Islamic world, into the Middle Ages and beyond. Though the path Galen cut had ultimately to be corrected, his writings dominated medical thought in the west for nearly a millennium and a half, from the 2nd century A.D. to the Renaissance.

Even that is not praise enough, for Galen was not merely a physician, but a philosopher. To be more exact, he entered into the medical debates of his day as both philosopher and physician. Consequently, his presentation of medicine is part of a larger argument about nature and human nature. When we seek to measure the influence of Galen on later generations, then, we find it not only in medicine, but in literature, art, philosophy, and theology as well.

What then did Galen think? Why was it so important? It is not my task in this introduction to provide an outline of Galen's thought, and thereby enter into a competition with the pages that follow. And happily so. As readers of Jeanne Bendick's delightful minor classic *Archimedes and the Door of Science* will readily agree, it would be a competition in which I could only hope to come in a distant second.

I do hope, however, to have whetted the reader's appetite. As should be evident by now, to be unfamiliar with Galen is to be ignorant of much that has moved and guided western thought. For this reason, Jeanne Bendick's *Galen and the Gateway to Medicine* is a most welcome book, one that should be on the shelf of every library as well as every serious home educator.

Yet Jeanne Bendick does much more than present the outlines of Galen's thought. She introduces the reader to Galen's thought through an engaging presentation of Galen the man. Even apart from the history of medicine, Galen's life is fascinating in and of itself. Imagine getting one's training as a doctor, by becoming a trainer and doctor of gladiators! Imagine pursuing one's medical education through perilous sea and land journeys! Imagine being the physician to Roman emperors!

Galen and the Gateway to Medicine could most accurately be described, then, as an adventure book—an adventure of medicine and philosophy not in some abstract sense, but as lived by the man whose adventure it was. It is written for the young, but as with Bendick's *Archimedes*, it is written so well, that teachers and parents will also delight in it and learn from it. That, as C. S. Lewis once said, is the sign of a truly good children's book.

Benjamin D. Wiker

Essay Questions for Student Writers

(1) Galen was the physician to the Roman emperor Marcus Aurelius. Marcus Aurelius was not only an emperor, but a famous philosopher as well. Find out what he believed and wrote.

(2) Marcus Aurelius was considered a wise and humane emperor. His son Commodus, however, was not. Find out some of the reasons for Commodus' bad reputation.

(3) Another very famous scientist, Claudius Ptolemaeus, was living about the same time as Galen. We call him "Ptolemy," and remember him primarily for his contributions to astronomy. Investigate Ptolemy's view of the universe, and how it differs from ours today.

(4) A famous Christian, St. Irenaeus, was also a contemporary of Galen. Write a short sketch of St. Irenaeus' life.

(5) Galen got his start as a physician to gladiators. Find out the names of Rome's most famous gladiators, and how they fought.

(6) Gaius Suetonius Tranquillus (70?-130?), known to us as Suetonius, was an historian who lived

when Galen was young, and wrote about the Roman emperors. What did he think about them?

(7) Of himself, Galen boasted "I have done as much for medicine as Trajan did for the Roman empire." Who was Trajan, and what did he do for Rome?

(8) After the time of Galen, no one rose to the stature of Galen as a physician until the Islamic physician and philosopher Avicenna, born near the end of the 10th century. What contributions to medicine did Avicenna make?

Who Was Galen?

Galen was a doctor who practiced medicine almost 2,000 years ago.

He was doctor to four Roman emperors, so Roman history could have changed if he made mistakes.

He was a doctor who tended the wounds of gladiators — wounds by sword, spear and the teeth of wild animals.

He was a doctor who had to learn about the human body from studying pigs and monkeys.

He was a doctor who invented and recorded so many medicines that some are still used today.

He was a doctor whose theories seemed so accurate that his ideas were taught and followed for almost 1,500 years.

He was Dr. Galen (GAY-len), the most famous doctor and scientist in the Roman empire.

Galen was born on September 22, in the year 129 (or maybe 130) in the Greek city of Pergamum (PUR-gum-um). In Galen's time, Greek people had only one name, but Romans had a string of names. The Roman emperor, in 129, was named Publius Aelius Hadrianus. But he is known, simply, as Hadrian. (HAY drey-an)

HADRIAN

About 250 years before Galen was born, the last ruler of Pergamum had given his city-state to Rome on the condition that Rome would protect its independence. But the people who lived there still considered it a Greek city.

By the time Galen was born, the Romans had conquered all the lands around the Mediterranean Sea, much of Europe (including England), part of Africa, the whole Middle East and some of Asia. If

you look at the map you can see how huge the Roman Empire was. You can see the city of Pergamum on the map, twenty miles from the Aegean (ih-JEY-en) Sea. (Today, Pergamum is called Bergama. It is in Turkey.)

What was so special about being a doctor in the second century? There were a lot of doctors then, but many of them had little medical training. A few did go to medical school. Others learned to be doctors by following other doctors around as apprentices, in much the same way as ironsmiths or weavers learned their trades. They learned by watching. There were no formal requirements for being a doctor — you just announced that you were one and that you were in the doctoring business. If you were fortunate enough to cure somebody you attracted more patients, otherwise you soon tried another profession.

Doctors might wander from place to place like traveling tradesmen. Some set up stalls in the marketplace, where they gave advice, sold cures, and offered first aid for simple problems.

In the second century people had many of the same health problems and diseases we have now, but there weren't many ways of treating them. Garlic and honey were the most trusted cures. Everyone ate garlic, raw and cooked. They drank garlic juice, rubbed it on, and wore garlic cloves around their necks. Honey was eaten, made into drinks, and smeared on wounds.

Doctors were only beginning to have ideas about what caused diseases. And even if they had known, they didn't have the medicines we have today. There were no vaccines, antibiotics, penicillin or sulfa drugs. There were no anesthetics. There wasn't even aspirin.

No one could see inside a living body.

X-rays and body scans were thousands of years in the future. It would be more than a thousand years before someone invented the thermometer for taking temperatures or the stethoscope for listening to hearts and lungs. Nobody had even invented a proper clock with which to time a pulse. (You couldn't time a pulse with a sun dial, a sand clock or a water clock.)

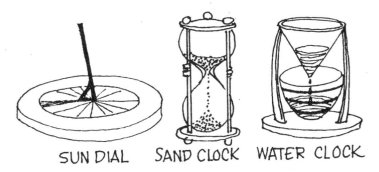

SUN DIAL   SAND CLOCK   WATER CLOCK

The workings of a human body were a mystery.

Was there some spirit inside that made people alive?

What, really, did the heart do? Did it control thinking? Or was it just a furnace to heat the blood?

Where did blood come from? How did blood begin? How did it move through the body? Were there different kinds of blood?

Where was air in the body? Was it in the veins? What did the lungs do? Did they cool the heart?

Did something in the liver make you brave?

Was gloominess centered in the stomach?

There was so much to figure out.

Galen's ambition was to learn everything about

the human body. He studied and taught and wrote about anatomy — how a body is made, how its parts are arranged and how the parts work together.

Galen believed that anatomy was the foundation of medical knowledge. But in Galen's time, dissection of humans — the cutting open of a dead body — was forbidden. This had not always been so, but now Greek religion said that dissecting dead people was dishonoring the dead. So most of what Galen knew about anatomy he learned from studying oxen and dogs, monkeys and pigs. Many of his ideas about how human body parts functioned were based on the animals he studied. (You can see how this led him to make some mistakes.)

For years, Galen was doctor to the gladiators who fought in the arena, so he learned a lot about treating wounds, broken bones and other physical injuries. He had good ideas, too, about how to keep those athletes healthy. He was an early expert in sports medicine.

As Galen learned more about doctoring, he thought of new ways to treat the diseases of his patients, experimenting to find cures for physical and even mental illnesses.

He mixed and measured and invented medicines from herbs and minerals, and he wrote down his prescription recipes and his advice on their use. He wrote thirty books on pharmacy — the science of preparing and prescribing drugs.

The Greeks loved science. They believed that an understanding of the world they lived in depended, first, on careful observations of the world around them. You had to gather the facts. (We call those facts data.)

You had to think about your data in an orderly way, and then you had to ask yourself questions about what those facts meant. (You can't get an answer before you ask a question. Scientists say that often questions are more important than answers.)

The answers are called a theory. A theory is an explanation of the facts, and the Greeks had theories about almost everything. Theories can change as new facts emerge because science is an ongoing search for truth.

Galen wanted to make medicine a science. He gathered, studied and summarized the ideas of the Greek scientists and physicians who lived before him. He was eager to connect known facts with his own ideas and he was sure he could do that in a logical way. He also wanted to separate superstition from real knowledge.

Galen was the most famous and important doctor of his time. He was also the most important doctor for almost fifteen centuries after he died.

During his lifetime he wrote more than three hundred books and articles. His writings were the most complete encyclopedia of medicine in the ancient world.

After he died, doctors still read his books and used his prescriptions. Scholars translated Galen's Greek writings into other languages. As centuries went on, medical schools all over Europe taught his theories. For almost 1,500 years most people believed that Galen had learned everything there was to know about medicine.

Galen's World

Galen was born to a wealthy family in Pergamum.

Galen's mother was famous for her temper. Her screaming and nagging could be heard up and down the street outside the house and she often bit her serving maids if they displeased her. Aside from her temper, nothing is really known about Galen's mother. Even her name is a mystery. Nobody knows, either, whether Galen had any brothers or sisters.

Galen's father, Nicon, (NEE-kon) really was famous as an engineer and architect. He was also a mathematician, a philosopher, an astronomer and a botanist.

Wealthy and important Greek and Roman citizens had time to do many things. They could spend as much time as they wanted reading, studying, discussing ideas and amusing themselves. Nicon probably got paid for designing buildings and engineering projects, but he never had to earn a living. He and his friends never had to help around the house, or take the children to school, or even dress themselves if they didn't want to. They had slaves to do all the work.

Many of the slaves were people who were captured when their countries lost a war. Slaves worked in houses, on farms and in mines. They

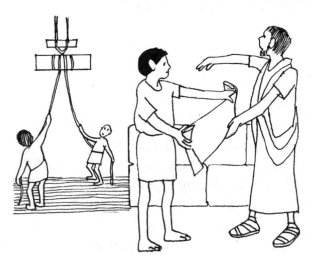

built roads, bridges and aqueducts. They were soldiers and policemen; they helped in shops, buried the dead, cleaned the streets and fought in the arena.

Rich people might own fifty slaves or five hundred or more. Some households had slaves who just took care of clothing, or who cooked only special dishes or did nothing but hairdressing. Educated slaves, especially those from Greece, were teachers, scribes, artists and craftsmen. They worked as clerks for the government. Some wrote plays and acted in them. Some did accounting and managed households. Some were doctors.

Children from wealthy families like Galen's were usually in the charge of their mothers and nurses until they were almost eight, but Galen was different. His father decided to be Galen's teacher and

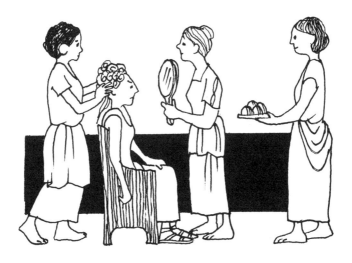

companion almost from the beginning. Probably, he wanted to keep him away from his bad-tempered mother.

Galen certainly had a slave to help him bathe and dress in his chiton, a simple robe made of linen in the summer or wool if the weather was cold. Galen's slave kept his things in order and taught him manners — how to behave in the proper Greek way.

Early in the morning Galen had breakfast in his room, usually bread, cheese and olives. If Galen had a sweet tooth, maybe he had honey on his bread — the Greeks didn't have sugar. The day started at sunrise and ended at  sunset. An hour was 1/12 of that time, so hours were of different lengths at different times of the year.

After breakfast, Galen and Nicon probably did lessons. And later they went together on errands around Pergamum.

Maybe they started at the agora, the great marketplace. Greek men often did the shopping, with slaves along to carry what they bought. There were acres of food in the stalls of the agora — fruits,

grains, eggs, vegetables, peas and beans. (No pota-
toes! No tomatoes! No corn! Those come from the
Americas and the discovery of America was more
than a thousand years in the future.) Nicon didn't
buy bread — that was baked by his own cooks in
his own kitchen. But poor people didn't have kitch-
ens, so they bought bread and whatever cooked
food they ate at the market. Only rich people
bought meat. Meat was very expensive and unless
it was fresh it was dangerous to eat because refrig-
eration hadn't been invented. Food spoiled quickly,
so funny tastes and smells were covered up with
very spicy sauces. You could buy those sauces in the
market.

Pergamum was a good place to grow up in. Many
years ago its rulers had made up their minds to

build a city more beautiful than Athens, the capital of Greece. So they designed grand palaces, houses and public buildings. They collected art from all over Greece to decorate their temples and public courtyards. Artists of Pergamum added their own work, carving statues, decorating walls with murals and floors with mosaic tiles. Silversmiths made fine things out of silver from the mines near the city. Galen was accustomed to having beautiful things around him.

Pergamum was built on a mountain. On the top were palaces and enormous temples to the important Greek gods, Zeus and Athena. Barracks for soldiers and arsenals for weapons were at the top, too.

There was a colosseum where gladiators fought in the arena—sometimes against each other, sometimes against wild animals.

Ten thousand people could watch plays in an open air theater. Often, Nicon and Galen sat on the stone benches of the theater and watched the actors, in their masks, perform the plays of famous Greek writers.

MASKS SHOWED WHO THE CHARACTERS WERE.
ALL THE ACTORS WERE MEN.

The streets and houses of Pergamum were built on great terraces going down the mountain. Important people like Nicon lived in spacious houses that looked out over the plain below. Poor people lived lower down in crowded tenements. Slaves lived in the houses of their masters.

Every day Nicon took Galen to the gymnasium. The Greeks loved gymnastics and they believed that everyone needed exercise to keep well. Galen learned to run and wrestle, to swim and throw the javelin. The gymnasium wasn't like any gym you've ever seen. It extended down three terraces of the city, all connected by covered marble staircases and passages. The gymnasium included training courts, a running track, a theater and two big baths. The baths weren't like anything you've ever seen, either.

There were hot rooms and cold rooms, hot pools and cold pools and places where men could just sit and talk. Women had their own, separate baths. There were steam rooms, saunas and wrestling rooms. Of course there were slaves to keep everything clean, stoke the fires for the hot water, hand out towels and serve snacks.

And then there was the library, which had more books than any library in the world except for the famous library at Alexandria, in Egypt. The books were all written by hand, on handmade paper. Then the sheets of paper were pasted together into long rolls called scrolls. Each scroll had its own case, a kind of tube with an open end.

Ptolemy I (TOL-um-ee), who became king of Egypt in 304 B.C., started the library at Alexandria. (Ptolemy had been one of Alexander the Great's best generals.) Ptolemy became so jealous of the library at Pergamum that he forbade Egypt

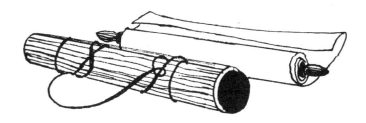

to export papyrus to Pergamum. Most books were written on paper made from papyrus, a reed that grew in Egypt, so Ptolemy hoped, by not allowing Pergamum to have paper, that the library wouldn't be able to add new books.

But scholars at Pergamum perfected a way to stretch and prepare animal skins — mostly cowhide — on which to write their books. (We call that "parchment." The word comes from the Latin word, "pergamena." Today, any good quality paper is called parchment.)

Stretched and cured animal skin had been used for writing since Biblical times, but "Pergamene paper" was thinner, smoother and easier to make in large sheets. It was a great improvement over papyrus paper which was fragile and apt to crumble as it got older. Now, not only were new books added to the Pergamum library, but parchment became an important export to cities all over the Empire.

While he was growing up, Galen couldn't use the library at Pergamum — it was for older students and scholars. But Nicon had his own library at home. It was a small room, but the walls were lined with cases containing rolls of books. Nicon probably had more than 1,000 scrolls. A slave kept the books in order and helped Galen when he was looking for a book to read.

Galen Goes
to School

When he was a little older, Galen went to school. Maybe you think that 2,000 years ago, in the second century, there wasn't a lot to learn. Well, what do you study?

Certainly you study your language. Galen learned to read and write Greek. He read and recited the works of Greek poets, so he learned to speak well in public. He learned Latin, too, since that was the Roman language.

Of course you learn mathematics. So did Galen. Greek and Roman numerals were difficult to do arithmetic with, but Galen used an abacus the way you may use a computer. Algebra hadn't been invented yet because nobody would think of the idea of zero for hundreds of years and you can't have algebra without zero. But geometry! The Greeks were wonderful at geometry. Galen studied straight lines and curved lines, arcs and circles, angles and triangles. He studied solids — spheres, cylinders, cubes and cones. Galen really loved geometry.

Euclid (YEW-klid), who lived from 330 B.C. until about 275 B.C., founded a famous school of mathematics at Alexandria. Euclid had a brilliant, orderly mind and he collected every fact that was known about geometry up to his time. He fitted them together as if

EUCLID

(NOBODY REALLY KNOWS HOW THESE ANCIENT GREEKS LOOKED.)

he were solving a giant puzzle and wrote every-thing down in thirteen books called *The Elements.*

Archimedes (Ark-i-ME-deez), who lived from 287 to 212 B.C., invented what we call "higher mathematics." He figured out how to measure figures drawn on flat surfaces and how to measure the volume of solids. He made discoveries about the elements, built machines, and worked with numbers too big to write down.

ARCHIMEDES

Galen studied science, too. The Greeks were fas-cinated by science, even though they didn't have any of the tools scientists have now. What they did have was curiosity and imagination.

They figured out a lot about astronomy more than a thousand years before Galileo made his dis-coveries with a telescope. They were sure that the earth was round and suspended in space, and they had the distance around the earth pretty well fig-ured out. They catalogued hundreds of stars and they knew that the planets were different from stars. They argued about the size of the sun and how far away it was, and they could predict eclipses.

Some ancient Greek scholars were convinced that everything was made of tiny particles they called atoms. And they knew something about magnetism, which they called, "elektron."

Galen studied history. Herodotus (Her-ODD-atus), who lived from 480 to 425 B.C., traveled everywhere in the ancient world known to the Greeks and wrote books about the cultures and histories of the places he visited. Herodotus is sometimes called The Father of History.

PLATO

All Greek boys studied the work of the great philosopher, Plato (PLAY-toe), who lived from 427 to 347 B.C. Plato founded a famous Academy of Learning in Athens. He believed that mathematics was the language of the universe.

Galen learned Plato's ideas about right and wrong, justice and law, and how hard it is to gain knowledge. But Plato believed that the human mind could gain absolute truth.

Plato's student, Aristotle (AR-is-TOTT- ul), was one of the greatest original thinkers of all time. Plato's search for truth inspired him. Aristotle, who lived from 384 to 322 B.C., mastered every field of learning known to the Greeks. He was a scientist, who observed and classified all the known plants and animals. He believed that all human knowledge begins with the experience of the senses — that you must look, listen, touch, smell and even taste to find out every possible thing about whatever it is you are studying.

ARISTOTLE

Aristotle was also a philosopher. Philosophy is the search for reality and the truth about life. The word "philosophy" comes from a Greek word meaning "love of wisdom."

Aristotle saw the universe as a world of perfect order, in which all things move toward God. He believed that happiness was the goal of life, but that pleasure, fame and wealth did not bring happiness. Aristotle said that only the understanding of truth brings happiness, because mankind's special talent is the use of reason. Galen made up his mind to search for truth, always.

Galen loved science. He loved philosophy. He loved studying. We don't know whether he loved going to the gymnasium or wrestling or swimming — maybe Nicon insisted that he do those things. Otherwise he would have spent all his time reading and writing. He wrote three books by the time he was thirteen.

When he was fourteen, Galen went to the School of Philosophy to study. Later he wrote that a good doctor had to be a philosopher, too. He worked so hard, so many hours a day, that he became tense and nervous. Nicon worried and urged him to go to the gymnasium to relax, but instead Galen did geometry. Galen's love of problems to solve lasted his whole life.

AESCULAPIUS

Galen Begins to Study Medicine

One of the grandest buildings in Pergamum was the Temple of Aesculapius (As-kul-APP-e-us), at the foot of the mountain.

Aesculapius was the Greek god of medicine. In myth, he was the son of Apollo, the god of truth and healing. Legend said that Aesculapius was the first physician — so skillful that he could bring the dead back to life.

There were other temples to Aesculapius but the one in Pergamum was the most famous. The temple had a sacred spring that started above ground and flowed into a large pool in an underground cavern beneath the temple. Drinking the waters from the spring, or bathing in the pool, was supposed to ease aches and pains. There were baths and mud baths, a library and a theater. In the temple itself there were rows of sleeping couches. The place for sleeping and dreaming was the most important part of the temple of Aesculapius.

People who were ill or in pain, depressed or upset, came to the temple for help. The temple priests, who were also doctors, moved among the patients, giving advice and some medicine. Tea, made from herbs and boiling water, was a universal treatment.

For headaches there was peppermint tea, for depression, clove tea, for anxiety, chamomile tea.

The priests even performed simple surgery. Generally, Greek doctors did not believe that most surgery was helpful — patients often died. (It wasn't understood, then, that surgical instruments had to be sterilized because they could carry deadly germs into a wound. Besides, a surgeon needs an accurate understanding of the human body and how it works. Doctors, then, did not have that knowledge.)

Patients in the temple listened to soft music, slept and dreamed. Their dreams were supposed to help them and their doctors understand what was wrong so they could be cured. Some dreams were supposed to come directly from Aesculapius, who performed miracle cures.

Other dreams were supposed to come from inside the patient. They would describe them to the doctors, who would interpret the dream and prescribe a cure.

Did the patient dream that a dragon with flaming breath was gnawing at his insides? He needed medicine to soothe his stomach — probably anise tea.

Did the patient dream that he was frightened and confused, surrounded by awful noises? The lyre player was summoned, along with a cup of chamomile tea.

People from all over the Roman province of Asia came to Pergamum's temple of Aesculapius to rest and dream.

Important people like judges, senators and even generals took turns serving as attendants in the temple as a way of performing social service. While he was in his teens, Galen served there too.

One day Nicon came to the temple and dreamed that Galen would be a great physician. He felt that Aesculapius had spoken to him. So when Galen was sixteen, his father persuaded him to study medicine.

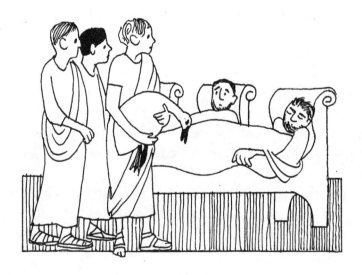

The Temple of Aesculapius was Galen's first medical school. His teachers, Satyrus (SAY-ta-russ) and Refinus (RAY-fin-uss), were among the important doctors who gathered there to study and treat the people who came for help. Part of the time, Galen and the other students simply followed their teachers around and watched as the doctors moved from patient to patient.

Sometimes the students carried the temple geese, which were encouraged to peck at boils until they burst. Once in a while, Galen held the leash of one of the temple dogs, who licked wounds to cure them. The doctors carried sacred snakes, too. (Statues of Aesculapius show him with a snake twined around his staff.)

At the Aesculapium, (As-kul-APP-e-um) teachers were the masters and the students were apprentices who learned on the job.

They were taught that the well-being and feelings of the patients were more important than what the students could learn about their diseases, and that careful, first-hand observation was better than book learning. Still, they studied the ideas of the medical thinkers who came before them.

They learned that there were three classes of living things: plants, animals and men.

Plants embodied the principle of growth. They were alive and they grew, but they couldn't move around.

Animals embodied the principle of growth + locomotion. They grew and they could move.

Men embodied the principle of growth + locomotion + reason. They grew, they could move, and they could think.

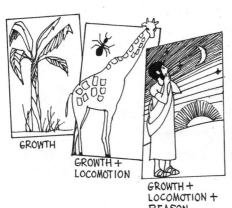

GROWTH

GROWTH + LOCOMOTION

GROWTH + LOCOMOTION + REASON

One of the most important ideas of Greek medicine was the concept of the pneuma (NOO-ma). The pneuma was a combination of breath — air breathed in — and vital spirit, which drifted through the universe. The pneuma made you alive. The Greeks thought that the pneuma was a real substance. But what created it? Galen and his friends argued endlessly over how the pneuma began.

Doctors and other scientists had been struggling for centuries to understand how the human body functioned. They had theories, but very little real knowledge about what caused diseases or what made people sick. They had only a few ideas about how to cure them.

Over centuries, many kinds of cures were tried. Those that worked were used again. Those that didn't work were abandoned. (Hopefully, patients were no worse for those cures.)

As they followed their teachers from patient to patient, Galen and the other students tried to recognize and describe the symptoms of diseases.

They took notes and compared their ideas with each other's and with those of their teachers. They recorded medical histories and watched, day by day, how symptoms changed. They recorded the patients' dreams.

From early times, Greek doctors had some of the best and simplest ideas — eat wisely, exercise regularly, keep clean, get plenty of sleep, and dream. From the time he was a student, Galen was interested in dreams as a help toward diagnosing a disease and curing it.

A student entering medical school today dives into an ocean of medical knowledge. The human body has been explored into its smallest cell. Genes that might cause diseases have been mapped. Viruses have been dissected. There are thousands of medicines to choose from. Millions of medical facts are only a computer's distance away and important medical news flashes around the world at the speed of light.

In Galen's day, even circulating ideas in a reasonable time was almost impossible. Doctors in Greece knew absolutely nothing about medicine in China or India. How could they know? Even around the Mediterranean Sea, communication from place to place was limited to slow travel by ship or caravan. There were no telephones, telegraphs, radios or computers. There were no airplanes or fast boats. A scroll, written by a doctor explaining his ideas, might take years to get from one place to another. In those times a place only a few hundred miles away was farther than the farthest place on earth is now.

Over time, though, the libraries in Pergamum and at the Aesculapium had been collecting the writings of the great Greek doctors who had lived before.

The students studied Aristotle, Galen's favorite philosopher-scientist. Aristotle, who was the son of a physician, saw life as a single process that began when a person was born and continued until he died. Aristotle thought that the heart was the seat of the mind.

They studied the ideas of Empedocles (Em-PED-uk-lez), who lived in Sicily in the fifth century B.C.

Empedocles developed a theory that all matter — everything that exists — was composed of four elements: fire, air, earth and water. It didn't matter if the thing was as simple as a stone or as complicated as a human, it was made of one or a combination of those four elements. Of course we know now that none of those things is an element. But for centuries this theory seemed to classify matter in an easy-to-understand way.

Four was an important number to the Greeks. They thought there were four primary colors: white, black, red and yellow.

There were four seasons.

There were four elements: fire, air, earth and water.

Each of those elements had a matching quality. Fire was hot; earth was cold; air was dry and water was wet.

Empedocles also said there were four humors, by which he meant liquids in the body. His four humors were blood, yellow bile, black bile and phlegm (flem), which is another name for mucus.

Each humor was associated with a particular organ of the body.

He matched everything up like this:

ELEMENT	QUALITY	HUMOR	WHAT ITS LIKE	SOURCE
FIRE	HOT	BLOOD	WET + HOT	HEART
AIR	DRY	YELLOW BILE	DRY + HOT	LIVER
EARTH	COLD	BLACK BILE	DRY + COLD	SPLEEN? STOMACH?
WATER	WET	PHLEGM	WET + COLD	BRAIN

He also said that each humor had its season, which made people feel in a particular way. Spring was the season of blood — it made you feel energetic and hopeful.

Summer was the season of yellow bile. It could bring disease. This seemed obvious because around the Mediterranean Sea, summer was the time of malaria.

Autumn was the season of black bile, which made you feel melancholy. Days were getting shorter and darker.

Winter was the time of phlegm, with coughs, colds and runny noses.

(The humors were very important, so more about them later.)

The students studied ideas from the great center of learning that Ptolemy I had established in Alexandria in 300 B.C. This was the same Ptolemy who was so jealous of his library. In addition to the library, there were schools of philosophy and science — mathematics and astronomy. The medical school there became the most famous in the ancient world around the Mediterranean Sea. The entire center of learning was called The Museum.

Erastistratus (Er-RASS-tis-TRA-tus), the leader of the medical school at Alexandria, believed that air was carried from the lungs to the heart, where it became vital spirit in the blood.

He also said that there were different kinds of nerves. Some sent signals to the muscles, which made you move. Others were connected to your senses. (We call those two kinds of nerves motor nerves and sensory nerves.)

Herophilus (Hir-OH-ful-us), who worked at Alexandria with Erastistratus (Isn't it lucky that those ancient Greeks had only one name?) distinguished between veins and arteries and realized that they both carried blood. This was an improvement on Aristotle's idea, that the arteries carried only air.

Herophilus also thought that the pulse began in the heart and that pulse rate was different if a person was well or ill. And he discovered that nerves in the eye were connected to the brain.

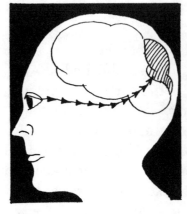

These two doctors had learned things that other doctors did not because, for just a few years, when they were at The Museum, dissection of human bodies was allowed. Then laws were passed to forbid it again and their writings were censored for hundreds of years. So it's possible that Galen studied their ideas, but we can't be sure.

There was one ancient doctor who was more important than all the others. Galen, the other students and the teachers revered him. His name was Hippocrates (Hip-POK-ra-teez), and he had been dead for almost 500 years.

HIPPOCRATES

About Hippocrates

Hippocrates was born about 460 B.C. on the Greek island of Cos (Kos). He was the son of a doctor named Heraclides (her-a-KLID-eez) and the grandson of a doctor who was also named Hippocrates. He seems to have come from a whole family of doctors. Hippocrates studied in Cos, then traveled all over Greece and Asia Minor, practicing medicine, teaching and writing. His school of medicine in Cos was famous in the ancient world and his writings have influenced doctors ever since. Hippocrates is often called "The Father of Medicine." Galen thought he was the perfect doctor and tried to model himself after him.

There are so many Hippocratic writings that historians think he couldn't have written all of them — that some were the work of his students and of other doctors who believed in the same things. And the writings extend over such a long period that if Hippocrates had written them all he would have lived to be 104 years old. One idea is that there were seven Hippocrates, all members of the same family, who did the writing.

Hippocrates said that there were three parts to human nature. Reason was in the brain; spirit was in the heart and appetites were in the liver.

Hippocrates agreed with Empedocles' ideas about the four humors. Did they know each other? Nobody knows. Maybe, while Hippocrates was traveling, the two doctors met and talked. In any case, Hippocrates was familiar with the four humors. He added his own ideas:

Each humor has its own effect on a person's health and even on the way he behaves.

Blood makes you lively.

Yellow bile makes you bold.

Black bile makes you downhearted and phlegm makes you slow.

Every person has his own balance of the mixture of humors, and good health depends on keeping that balance. When the balance is upset, you become ill.

Hippocrates' ideas about the humors seem odd to us

39

now, even though it's true that people do have certain personality traits. But the humors were the last word in medicine for more than a thousand years. Galen based much of his own work on Hippocrates' ideas and he promoted and discussed them in his own writing. Galen believed that Hippocrates was the fountain of all medical knowledge. He also thought that Hippocrates was a lot like himself.

Hippocrates said that a doctor needed to know his patient's way of life — what he ate, where he worked and where he lived — that a doctor must understand a person's environment. That really was a sound idea, because, for example, malaria was epidemic in low-lying, marshy Greece. What he didn't understand was the role of mosquitoes. But it would not be very long before the Romans sensed that something in the marshes carried diseases.

Hippocrates said that there were two kinds of illness — one of the body and one of the mind. There is a story that he cured the King of Macedon of a long illness that was thought to be consumption (tuberculosis) by recognizing that the king was suffering in his mind, from depression.

But Hippocrates was also a great believer in astrology, the belief that the sun, the moon, the stars and the planets had power over people's health. He said that a physician without a knowledge of astrology had no right to call himself a physician.

Probably the most important thing that Hippocrates taught was a code of medical ethics — his ideas about the relationship between doctors, their patients and their profession. His students made certain promises when they finished their training. The Hippocratic Oath has changed somewhat over these thousands of years, but some medical schools still use it. The original oath went something like this:

"I do solemnly swear by Apollo The All-Healer:

That I will be loyal to the profession of medicine and just and generous to its members;

That I will lead my life and practice my art in uprightness and honor;

That into whatsoever house I shall enter, it shall be for the good of the sick to the utmost of my power, holding myself aloof from wrong, from corruption, and from the temptation of others to vice;

That I will exercise my art solely for the cure of my patients. I will give no deadly medicine to anyone if asked, nor suggest any such counsel; and in like manner I will not give to a woman anything to produce an abortion.

That whatsoever I shall see or hear of the lives of men which is not fitting to be spoken, I will keep inviolably secret.

These things I do promise, and in proportion as I am faithful to this my oath may happiness and good repute be ever mine — the opposite if I shall be forsworn."

It is quite likely, when he finished his studies in Pergamum, that Galen took the Oath of Hippocrates.

Galen's Travels

When Galen was 19, just after he finished studying at the Aesculapium, his father, Nicon, died. Now Galen was very rich and very lonely. Everything in Pergamum reminded him of his father and he wanted to get away. Why not travel, he thought, and continue studying medicine in other places?

He had met Pelops (PAY-lops), a famous doctor, when he lectured in Pergamum. Pelops lived in Smyrna (SMUR-nuh), a few days' journey south of

Pergamum. So Galen decided to go to Smyrna and then, maybe, to move on from there.

He could do whatever he wanted to do. He didn't have to worry about his house; there were plenty of slaves to take care of it and a good household manager to run things. He would take a few of his favorite slaves and a few personal belongings with him. (Later, he said that he could go anywhere in the world with two slaves, two changes of clothing and a few pots and pans.)

Smyrna is only about 75 miles from Pergamum, but in Galen's time that wasn't an easy trip to make.

The Romans had built wonderful roads to connect the important cities in their empire. The roads were stone, set in concrete (an invention of the Romans) with curbstones and drainage canals. They were grand roads, wide and straight, so Roman

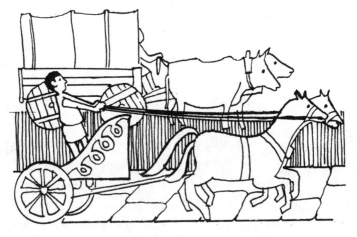

armies could move swiftly. Where there were rivers, they built stone bridges. Where there were valleys, they crossed them with giant viaducts. (Many of those roads, bridges and viaducts are still there.)

They also built very good smaller roads so government officials, tax collectors and messengers carrying mail could get from place to place, quickly. Important people and business travelers also rode in the mail coaches.

Two-wheeled chariots and four-wheeled coaches were allowed on the road, but the road keepers frowned on slow, heavy wagons carrying freight. When it was possible, freight traveled by boat and the roads were for people.

Maybe Galen traveled to Smyrna in a litter, a kind of couch with an awning and side curtains, carried on the shoulders of his slaves. Rich or important people did not walk on long journeys. Probably he rode in a four-wheeled carriage, pulled by

horses. The carriage was big enough to carry his baggage and his slaves. It was also big enough for him to sleep in along the way, unless he could stop at the houses of Nicon's friends.

The journey took several days and any inns on the road were terrible. Innkeepers were not to be trusted; the inns were hangouts for crooks and cutthroats; the food was awful and the bedding, which was hardly ever changed, was infested with insects. Besides, there were often bandits on the roads. In Galen's time, people did not travel for pleasure.

When Galen reached Smyrna, he stayed with Pelops, along with the other medical students at Pelops' school. He studied philosophy as well as medicine, and botany, which is the science of plants.

In the first century, a Greek physician and botanist named Dioscorides (dis-KO-rid-eez) described 600 plants, along with some minerals that he thought were helpful as medicine. His book, *De Materia Medica*, was the first known textbook of pharmacology. Dioscorides had traveled with the armies of the Roman emperor Nero, and the use of plants to cure illness became his passion.

He also invented a remedy he called oxymel, made of honey and cider vinegar, which became a famous cure for everything from allergies to arthritis.

Botany fascinated Galen, so whenever he could, he took time off to travel around the Province of Asia, investigating and collecting the plants people were using as medicine.

Galen stayed with Pelops for a while, then he became restless. He felt that it was time to move on, this time to Corinth, on the mainland of Greece, to continue his studies. He had no responsibilities and no one to please but himself.

Besides, he was interested in seeing more of the world. So far in his life Smyrna was the only place he had seen beyond Pergamum.

Going to Corinth meant making a sea voyage across the Aegean Sea.

If you look at the map you can see that most of the important cities around the Mediterranean are seaports. Since earliest times, trade among those cities had been sea trade. For centuries, ships had

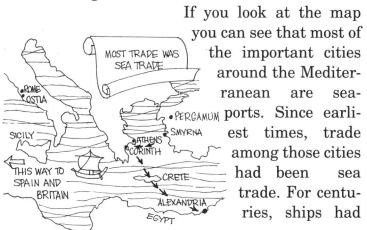

carried wheat, wood, and marble from Egypt; glass and pottery, wine and oil from Greece; fruit from Persia; metal from Spain and even, lately, tin from Britain.

Except for small fishing boats, ships were either warships or merchant ships. Warships had small sails, but usually they were powered by banks of rowers, pulling on oars. Sometimes there were two, or even three levels of rowers. Merchant ships were sail powered. There were no passenger ships.

Galen had to wait in Smyrna for a merchant ship, bound for Corinth, that would give him passage. Depending on the time of year, the wait might be long — winter in the Aegean Sea was stormy and the waters were rough and dangerous. Besides, in those times, ships could sail only before the wind, so winds had to be blowing in the right direction. Very few captains took their ships to sea from September until the middle of March.

WAR SHIP

CARGO SHIP

Galen finally sailed on a stubby cargo ship packed with clay jars of olive oil from the Greek island of Lesbos. The huge jars were packed into the hold in layers three or four jars deep. The captain and Galen slept in a cabin on the deck. The crew and Galen's slaves slept out under the stars. Sometimes Galen joined them.

Nobody is sure just how long Galen studied in Corinth, but he got restless there, too. He still wasn't satisfied with what he was learning. But where to? There was only one answer. He would go to Alexandria, in Egypt, to the great learning center called The Museum.

Again, Galen waited in the port, for a ship that would take him to Alexandria. Finally, he met the captain of a cargo ship that had delivered its load of Egyptian wheat to Corinth. Almost all the wheat for Rome and its provinces came in a steady stream of ships across the Mediterranean from Egypt.

The grain ship was much bigger than the little round ship that had carried Galen from Smyrna. (In Galen's time, 65 feet was a very big ship.) Still, it was a long, rough voyage. There were no compasses and no sea charts. Captains steered by the stars and relied on their own experience and the stories of other captains. Where were the best winds? Where were the reefs? Where were pirates most likely to be lurking? We know now that thousands of ancient ships were wrecked during their voyages across the Mediterranean. The sea floor there is still littered with them.

The ship stopped at the island of Crete for fresh water, raisins and almonds, fruit and vegetables.

Galen paid for new supplies. He loved good food, and there wasn't much on the ship but dried salt fish and hard bread.

While he was in Crete, Galen roamed the hills, collecting herbs for his medicine box. He told the captain that the only way to learn about plants was to study them directly — nobody could learn botany from books.

And maybe, always curious, he had a chance to explore the ruins of the great palace of King Minos, which had been destroyed by earthquakes more than a thousand years before. The palace had hundreds of rooms, and there were legends that the Minatour had lived there, below the palace.

Days later, the ship sailed past the giant lighthouse at Pharos, into the harbor at Alexandria. The docks and the harbor stretched in all directions, crowded with ships from everywhere, loaded with everything. Caravans from China and India had brought silk, cotton and spices for the markets of the Empire. Grain from all over North Africa and Egypt was being loaded. Pottery and wine were being unloaded. Laborers were shouting, the sun was hot, the air was filled with unfamiliar smells.

Once ashore, he was in a crowd of merchants and slaves, tourists, shoppers and scholars — Egyptians, Greeks, Romans and Hebrews, Arabs, Nubians, Persians and Phoeniceans. Alexandria!

For the first time, Galen stopped missing his father and worrying about himself and his future. He was excited and ready for anything. On to The Museum!

Alexandria!

Galen hurried through the crowded streets toward The Museum — he could see the buildings
ahead of him. On the way, he heard a dozen languages and he saw a dozen kinds of people he had
never seen before. He smelled a hundred kinds of
smells from stalls selling foods he could not even
imagine.

The Museum was immense, spreading out
around the royal palace. The buildings were grand.

There was the library, of course — maybe several libraries. There were lecture halls and a tall observatory. Were those laboratories over there? And he could hear the noise from the zoo. It had animals from all over the empire — lions, cheetahs, antelopes, oxen, giraffes, wild pigs, ostriches, and several kinds of monkeys.

He could see sleeping halls and dining halls and he walked through a beautiful park. Some people strolled the paths. Others sat on stone benches, talking or just thinking.

Teachers and students, playwrights and poets, people who wrote history and people who wrote philosophy worked and studied and lived at The Museum. There were mathematicians and astronomers. There were historians, studying the past and arguing about what that meant to the future. There were geographers, trying to figure out what the earth was like. There were doctors and medical students trying to figure out what the human body was like.

They came together from all over the ancient world, living together, eating together, arguing with each other. The Museum at Alexandria was a kind of giant university.

From the beginning, Galen felt at home. He was always impatient with people who, in his opinion, didn't use their minds, so he was happy to be with so many serious scholars.

He and his friend Ptolemy, (who wasn't related to the king) compared notes about their futures. Ptolemy wanted to map the world. Galen wanted to map the human body.

"I am going to travel the earth," Ptolemy said. "And make a map showing land and water, where they begin and where they end, and their relationship to each other."

"I am going inside the human body," Galen said. "And map the parts and show their relationship to each other."

They spent hours arguing over which was most important.

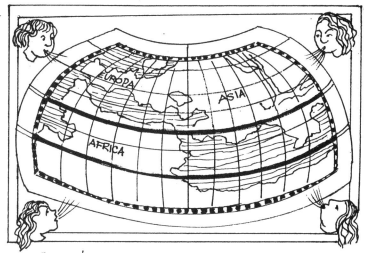

PTOLEMY'S MAP OF THE WORLD WAS LOST. BUT IN THE 15TH CENTURY SCHOLARS USED HIS INSTRUCTIONS TO RECREATE IT.

Ptolemy went on to become famous, too. He wrote *The Almagest*, a digest of all Greek astronomy, but his greatest work was in geography. His map of the world used latitude and longitude for the first time. And he made his own projection, which showed the spherical world on a flat page. Ptolemy's geography was called *Geographia*.

Galen spent hours in the vast libraries. There were more than half a million books — all copied by hand, of course. He read the original texts of the great Greek writers. He read Greek translations of the Old Testament. There were even thousands of books that had been looted from the Pergamum library a couple of hundred years earlier. Marc Antony had taken them to give to Cleopatra, Queen of Egypt, as a present.

Dissection of humans was still forbidden, but now, for the first time, Galen was able to study a human skeleton. There were two at The Museum. One had been stripped clean by vultures; the other had been washed clean by the Nile. Galen was astonished by the wonderful architecture of those skeletons.

He admired the vertebrae — the twenty-four bones of the back, which made the body flexible. He

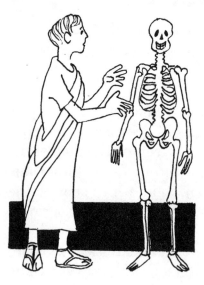

admired the ribs, the flat bones which protected the organs, and the long, hollow bones of the arms and legs. Where bones came together he examined the joints, and figured out which were designed to move and which did not. He admired the way the bones of the skull fitted together and how the teeth were adapted to different kinds of chewing. (Galen considered the teeth as bones.) He believed that every detail demonstrated the perfect design of a Creator he called Nature.

But he could tell only so much from bones. How were they connected, so that a body could move and bend? So a hand could grasp and pick things up? How did a throat swallow? How did a tongue move to talk? Galen needed to study muscles. He couldn't do that from a skeleton.

He had to dissect animals. Galen was sure that the bodies of animals were similar to the bodies of people, even though their shapes might be different. The medical students at the Museum were allowed to dissect some of the animals in the zoo for their studies.

Galen dissected pigs and an ox. He compared the throats of an ostrich and a crane. He felt that his best subjects were Barbary apes (which were actually monkeys,) because they were most like humans.

He loved anatomy, the study of any living thing's structure. All the parts of a plant or an animal make up its anatomy. Galen thought that anatomy was the foundation of medical knowledge. And the science that explains the functions of all those parts and the connections between them is called physiology.

From his careful dissections and observations, Galen began to ask himself questions and to form his own ideas. To begin with, he thought the body had three connected systems. (These ideas began with Aristotle.)

The liver and the veins were responsible for nutrition and growth, which he called natural spirit.

Life-giving energy, which he called vital spirit, was carried out by the heart.

Sensation and intelligence, which he called animal spirit, were the job of the brain.

You can follow Galen's ideas on this diagram he made.

One of Galen's most important contributions was in trying to put these processes in order.

First, where did blood come from? And how was it made?

He decided that blood must begin with food and that the liver changed food into blood. (He said that natural spirit began in the liver.) Then, blood moved from the liver through the veins to nourish every part of the body.

He said that blood from the liver must go first to the heart. It came to the right ventricle of the

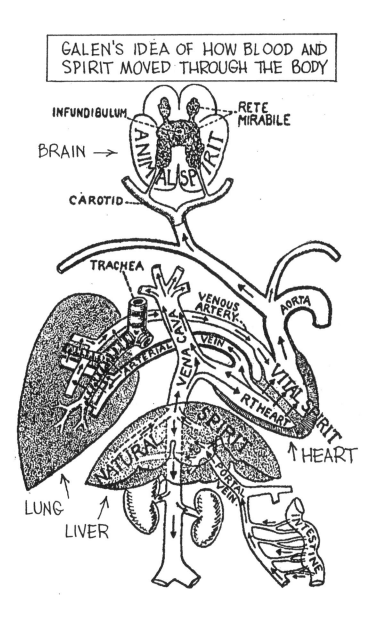

GALEN'S IDEA OF HOW BLOOD AND SPIRIT MOVED THROUGH THE BODY

heart, where it got rid of impurities and was lightened into a kind of froth before going to the lungs. (In his dissections, Galen could see the honeycomb appearance of the lungs and they seemed too delicate to handle ordinary blood.)

Then, the blood goes from the right side of the heart to the left side. But how could it do that? The wall between the right ventricle and the left ventricle looked solid. Galen decided that there must be pores for the blood to seep through. He had no microscope, so he had no way to check this idea, so Galen imagined the pores. They don't exist, but he couldn't think of any other way to get blood from the right side of the heart to the left. The wall between them is solid.

In the left ventricle, he said, the blood was mixed with air containing pneuma, which was breathed in by the lungs. Now, the blood, joined to the pneuma, became vital spirit that flowed through arteries to all parts of the body. So while the veins contained only blood, the arteries contained blood and air + pneuma.

Some arteries led to the brain. There, a network of tiny blood vessels, which Galen said he saw, passed the blood into the brain where it became animal spirit. (These tiny blood vessels do exist in hoofed animals, but not in humans. Galen may have seen them in his dissections of sheep and pigs.) Finally, the nerves sent that combination of blood and animal spirit through the body.

Galen, asking himself questions and trying to find logical answers, was sure that this system was true.

He thought that three different kinds of blood, each carrying its own spirit, did different kinds of work in the body. He had no way of knowing that an animal has only one kind of blood, moving in a continuing circle, in one direction, pumped by the heart. (It would be almost 1,500 years before anyone figured that out.) Galen understood that blood moved, but he did not know how. He thought it might ebb and flow, like the tide.

Galen was trying to put together what he observed into a theory that explained how the parts of the human body functioned together as an interconnected system.

Even though he was studying and experimenting, Galen began to be dissatisfied with his work at Alexandria.

Galen had been away from Pergamum for nine years. He decided that the time had come for him to stop being a student and begin to be a doctor.

Galen and
the Gladiators

Galen was happy to return to Pergamum. He had his house and his friends — his fellow students and his teachers from the Aesculapium. He had his father's friends, too, who wanted to help him make a place for himself. One of them owned the ludi, the school for gladiators that was attached to the gymnasium and the arena.

The school needed a new doctor. It was just the right moment for Galen and he was just the right person for the job.

Gladiators were the professional athletes of Galen's time, and for hundreds of years before and after. But most of them had not chosen the profession.

Some were prisoners of war, or likely looking slaves who had been bought because they looked like good fighters. Some were condemned criminals. The promising ones, who had committed only petty crimes, were trained as gladiators. (Murderers and traitors were sent into the arena with no training and without weapons.)

In the ludi, gladiators-in-training became specialists in different kinds of combat. They could choose the weapons and armor and the kind of fighting that suited them best — something like choosing courses at school.

You could choose to fight with a long, oblong shield, a plumed, visored helmet and a short sword or two. You could choose a heavy, round shield and a long, curved dagger. Or you might want to fight with only a huge net, in which to tangle your opponent and a trident with which to puncture him after he was caught. You could learn to fight with a heavy chain or a lasso.

If you had been a horseman, you might want to fight blindfolded on horseback. If you had been a soldier, you might choose to fight other gladiators as you galloped past each other in chariots.

There were also free men who volunteered to be gladiators simply because they liked to fight. Some of them made a great deal of money. The prizes for popular gladiators were huge and they became local or national heroes.

Gladiator fighting was the most popular sport in the Roman empire, even more than chariot racing. (You needed a huge stadium to race chariots, but even a small city could afford gladiators and an arena.) The largest arenas were like the biggest football stadiums today, except that the seats were usually made of stone. The Colosseum in Rome could seat 50,000 people. (Once, the emperor Titus put on a show where 5,000 pairs of gladiators fought each other.)

Gladiators didn't fight just other gladiators in the arenas. They fought wild beasts — lions and panthers, bears, bulls, rhinos, crocodiles and even hippopotamuses.

Watching gladiators fight with each other and with savage animals was part of being a Roman. War and bloodshed were part of Roman life. Being wounded or killed was part of being a gladiator. Slaves and criminals who survived three years of combat could earn their freedom. They were only required to fight two or three times a year, but very few made it.

Galen was eager to start work; he signed a contract. Sports medicine was going to be his job for the next three years. The gladiators had already taken an oath to be slaves to the owner of the school, "to endure branding, chains, flogging, or death by the sword."

Galen was more than a doctor and surgeon to the Pergamum gladiators. First, he was their trainer. The men in the school lived in barracks attached to the arena. He saw that they had good food and enough sleep. He supervised their exercise. He watched them run and wrestle. He watched them take lessons in rope throwing and net throwing, in using swords, maces, tridents and heavy staffs. Their teachers were experienced gladiators who were either owned by or paid by the master of the school.

The teachers were strict and tough — after all, the students would be fighting for their lives when they entered the arena. If they lost a match, they would die. So even in training, bones were broken, jaws, knees and shoulders were dislocated, heads were banged and blood flowed from wounds.

The first remedy for sprains and bruises was a cloth soaked in cold water.

Sometimes, wounds were washed with red wine. It was an antiseptic, although the Greeks didn't know that word, or even why the red wine worked. Honey was used on almost all wounds. It was a disinfectant and an antibiotic, although ancient doctors didn't know those words, either. (Honey breaks down into hydrogen peroxide.) But doctors knew that honey helped healing. The Egyptians used honey in 500 of their 700 cures.

Galen was busy. He had assistants to help him, slaves and, probably, students from the Aesculapium. If they were resetting a dislocation, the assistant held the patient, while Galen used his hands to push the joint back into place.

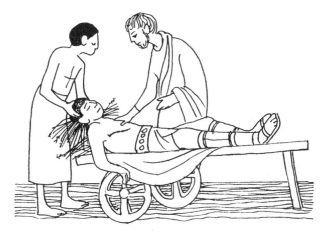

Galen set broken bones with smooth splints of different lengths, and with yards and yards of soft clean bandages, three or four fingers thick. First he bandaged from the injury up. Then he bandaged from the injury down. Then he bandaged over the break itself. Finally he rubbed a soothing cerate (SER-at) of oil mixed with wax into the folds of the bandage.

Once real fighting began, the wounds were much more serious, even if you were the winning gladiator. Sometimes, if you were the loser, you were dead. Usually, if you were brave, the crowd gave you a "thumbs up," which meant, "Let him live." Gladiators were important sports heroes.

Galen and his helpers cleaned out wounds, and sewed them up. But while he was working on the wounds, Galen had a chance to study the nerves, muscles and tendons under the skin. He also observed that when one side of the brain was damaged by a terrible blow, the opposite side of the body was paralyzed.

In cases when wounds were really severe, Galen could see the gladiator's organs — how they were placed in relation to each other. And once, when a young gladiator received a terrible chest wound, Galen observed his beating heart. Galen said

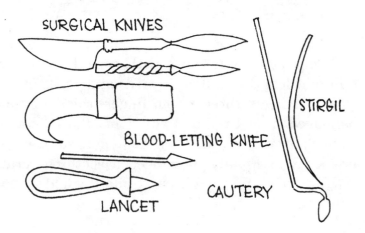

SURGICAL KNIVES

BLOOD-LETTING KNIFE

LANCET

CAUTERY

STIRGIL

wounds were his windows into the body, a first-hand look at human anatomy.

He had well-made surgical tools to work with, made by excellent craftsmen, who used iron, steel and bronze, silver, bone and sometimes ivory. Here are some of his tools:

Several shapes of surgical knives for cutting into the body. They had steel or bronze blades, with bumpy handles to provide a secure grip.

A blood-letting knife. Bleeding was supposed to get rid of poisons in the blood.

A lancet for letting blood out and for opening abcesses.

A cautery, which was heated to burn away infection or to stop bleeding.

A drill to remove a weapon lodged in a bone.

A steel chisel to divide a twisted bone.

Several kinds of forceps and a bone saw.

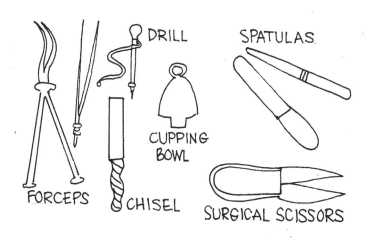

A stirgil, ordinarily used for scraping oil and sweat off the body after exercise, was handy for getting into small places, such as the ear.

A cupping bowl, which was applied to the skin to relieve local congestion or inflamed tissues.

Spatulas for spreading healing or pain-killing ointments.

Surgery worked well on arms and legs if the patient was brave and the doctor had good tools and a lot of experience. In his four years as physician to the gladiators, Galen did get a lot of experience, but when his contract was up in the autumn of the year 161 he decided that it was time to move on, even though he also had many private patients in Pergamum.

Galen was 31 years old and very ambitious. Pergamum was a great city, but it was not the greatest city. He felt that he belonged in Rome.

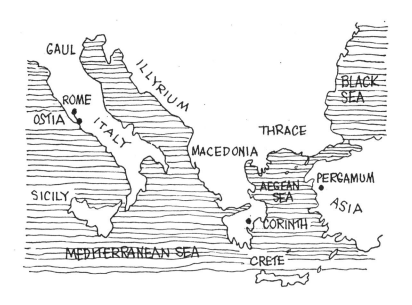

Galen Goes
to Rome

It took Galen almost a year to travel from Pergamum to Rome. If you look at the map, maybe you can figure out how he traveled, by land and sea, to get there. It was not an easy journey. Maybe he arrived at Ostia, which was the port of Rome — all sea trade for Rome came into Ostia.

71

If they came by sea, Galen, his slaves and their baggage came up the river from Ostia to Rome. If they came by land, they probably traveled along the grand highway called the Appian Road.

Galen went immediately to the house of Eudemus (YEW-duh-mus), his father's friend and his own old philosophy teacher. But Eudemus wasn't feeling well, so he sent Galen along to other friends of Nicon.

Galen needed advice on where to live.

He had passed through the narrow streets that wound between the seven hills of Rome. Some streets were crowded with four-story apartment

houses where workers, tradesmen and craftsmen lived, but he didn't want to live there. He had passed an area of much nicer apartment houses, and of pleasant, small houses, close together, but he didn't want to live there, either. His father's friends advised him to look for a house in the hills.

While he was settling in, Galen explored Rome. He was used to big cities; he had lived in Pergamum and Alexandria. But now, Rome was the chief city of the world and it astonished him.

Sometimes he traveled in a litter, but in the most crowded parts of Rome he went on foot. Carts were forbidden in the streets from daybreak until dusk — that law had been made because the carts caused such traffic jams that people couldn't get through to do their errands.

He went to the Circus Maximus where the chariot races were held and he went to the Colosseum, which made the arena in Pergamum seem tiny. Entertainment in Rome wasn't mainly for the rich. It was for the amusement of the mobs — people who were very poor and likely to riot unless they were kept entertained and given food. Most seats in the arena were free, and every day, bread was given to the unemployed.

He rode in his litter along the Sacred Way, past the temples to the gods and he passed the mighty arches built by past emperors to celebrate Roman victories.

He liked going to the Forum, an immense plaza which was surrounded by the grand marble buildings of the government. The Forum was always crowded — it was the main marketplace and the business center of Rome. People came to do their shopping and banking. Senators hurried in and out of the buildings. Lawyers and their clients were on their way to the law courts. Almost everyone stopped, for a little while, to listen to the orators who were making speeches and presenting their opinions on events in the empire.

People were shopping for bread and groceries. They were buying pots and plates, olive oil, vegetables, grain and maybe a little meat. Shoppers didn't argue about weight and price — government inspectors made regular visits to check that scales were accurate, prices were fair and the quality was good. Some food prices were set by law.

In the most crowded parts of the city, the streets were lined with apartment buildings. Many shopkeepers owned their own stores and lived in the apartments above them. City water was piped to the first floors, but had to be carried upstairs in buckets.

The Romans had advanced ideas about sanitation. They felt that clean water was necessary to good health and they built great aqueducts to carry pure water from the countryside into Rome, where there was a good sewage system and excellent public and private baths. The Romans loved being clean. Galen approved of that.

The baths in Pergamum didn't compare to the baths in Rome, where the walls were mirrored, the ceilings were glass and the pools were lined with marble. Beautiful mosaics tiled the floors.

The baths had libraries, restaurants, taverns, and stalls where hot sausages and cakes were sold. There were shops, theaters and even museums. Most Roman baths were free, but the fanciest ones charged a small fee to keep out slaves and poor people.

From all over the Empire, professional people came to Rome. Businessmen. Soldiers. Gladiators. Lawyers. Doctors.

Once, the Romans had disliked doctors. They thought that a family should do its own healing, helped by herbs and magical charms. Most of the early doctors in Rome were freed Greek slaves and

they were regarded as "quacks," or fakes. There was a Roman saying, "Beware of doctors — they bring death by medicine."

The Romans began to accept doctors in the first century B.C., when a Greek doctor named Asclepiades (As-kle-PIE-ah-des) arrived in Rome, saying that disease should be treated safely, speedily and above all, agreeably. Now, educated doctors served the rich, and less learned doctors had the poor as patients.

There were doctors for every part of the body and for every organ of the body. There were skillful, educated doctors and doctors who had no training at all. Some relied only on astrology, some on medicines and cures of their own invention. Some had stalls in the marketplace, others had grand homes.

Galen was worried. How was he going to make his name among so many doctors?

His fame began with his father's friend, Eudemus, who was getting sicker and sicker, even though his doctor was one of the most important in Rome. Eudemus sent for Galen, who examined him carefully, made his own diagnosis, and prescribed treatment and medicine, which he made himself. Eudemus recovered and suddenly important people all over Rome wanted Galen to be their doctor.

The important people were not only those who were rich, or who were government officials. Orators and architects, philosophers and lawyers, astrologers and famous athletes were equals in Rome.

One of the important people was the consul, Flavius Boethius (FLAY-vi-us Bo-EE-thee-us), whose wife was ill. When Galen cured her, Boethius became his greatest fan. He paid Galen a fee of 400 gold pieces for the cure.

Boethius insisted that Galen give lectures to explain his ideas, even arranging a lecture hall so the public could listen to him. He also established a large dissecting room, well-lit by torches, where Galen could perform public dissections of animals. (The dissection of a live animal is called vivisection.) Both the lectures and the dissections became popular entertainments among the educated people in Rome.

In one demonstration, Galen wanted to prove that speech came from the brain, not the heart, even though sound seems to come from the chest. (The ancient doctors thought that thinking, too,

came from the heart.) He tied off the vocal chords of a live pig and immediately the loud squeals stopped. When he released the ties the pig began to squeal again, so Galen had proved an important point.

In another demonstration he showed that the arteries carried blood, not just air. It had been thought that the veins carried blood through the body, while the arteries were supposed to carry vital spirit from the heart. Galen tied off the artery of an animal in two places so blood could not flow into the artery. Then he made a deep cut between the ties and blood spurted out. He had made another point.

Sometimes Galen explained an experiment while assistants did the cutting. Usually, though, he became impatient with them and took over the operation himself.

In still another demonstration he showed the importance of the spinal cord — that wherever it was severed, there would be no movement in the part of the body below the cut. But if the cord was severed at the fourth vertebra or above it, death was immediate.

He used dogs to demonstrate how kidneys and bladders functioned. (Humans are different, but Galen had no way to know that.)

These demonstrations seem cruel to us, but to the Romans they were simply fascinating scientific experiments. Now we know how each demonstration expanded the understanding of how different parts of the body functioned.

Galen's medical lectures drew bigger and bigger audiences. He was an excellent speaker and found words to explain scientific ideas in ways that his audience could understand. He stated his own views confidently and didn't hesitate to mock other doctors for their greed, ignorance, and pretended knowledge of the art of medicine. He said that some doctors were more famous for their wealth than for  their skill. Of course the doctors he made fun of hated him and there were loud public quarrels. Galen got into so many quarrels, and made so many enemies, that often he apologized. He said, publicly, "I'm sorry. I will never do that again." (But he did.)

While he was lecturing and demonstrating, he was also writing books, articles, and "guidebooks" for doctors whom he felt lacked proper knowledge. He wrote so much that he employed twenty scribes to keep up with his work. Remember, every word had to be written by hand, first on clay tablets, then on paper or parchment. After that, the text was given to a Scriptorium where other scribes copied it into books to be sold to the public.

And of course, he had patients. First and always, Galen was a doctor.

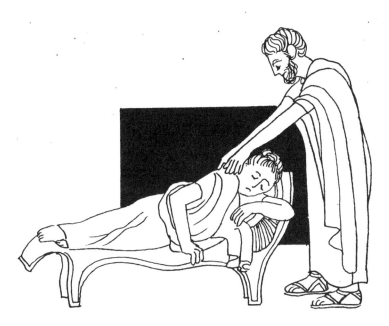

Doctor Galen's Medicine

Galen became the most famous doctor in Rome. He was doctor to the new emperor, Marcus Aurelius (Uh-REE-lee-us), and his co-emperor, Lucius Verus (VAY-rus). Later, he was also doctor to Marcus' young son, Commodus (Co-MOW-dus). His other patients were senators, consuls, orators, architects, engineers and most of the aristocrats of Rome. He once wrote that he succeeded because he called on the mighty in the morning and dined with them in the evening. He also said that a doctor was more useful if he was a friend than a stranger.

Galen enjoyed being a center of public attention, but being famous wasn't why he had so many important people as patients. They chose him because he was a very good doctor.

The best doctors were highly respected among educated, aristocratic Romans. The common people distrusted them, but they didn't have access to those doctors, anyway— they were much too expensive. Galen's fees were high. He also charged for a consultation by letter, even if he didn't visit the patient. Doctors usually made house calls.

A slave would summon Galen to the home of the patient. Galen probably arrived in his litter, accompanied by an assistant who carried any instruments Galen might need, along with a tablet for taking notes.

Galen's examination was careful. He had no thermometer, but he could feel a fever. He had no stethoscope but he understood heart sounds. He could feel a pulse; he understood changes from the ordinary rhythms.

Was the pulse irregular, or very fast?

Was the patient too pale? Too red? Breathing badly? Was any part of the body swollen? Sensitive to touch?

He dictated the patient's symptoms to his assistant. He listened to complaints and asked a lot of questions. When did the symptoms start? What had the patient been doing and where had he been before he felt ill? What had he had to eat or drink?

Today, when doctors are diagnosing a disease — deciding what is wrong with a patient — they have a lot of help. They begin by knowing what the possibilities are. They have learned long lists of symptoms attached to known diseases. They can recognize even small symptoms, maybe an odd headache, or a faint rash. Symptoms of even rare diseases can be matched on a computer. X-rays, MRIs,

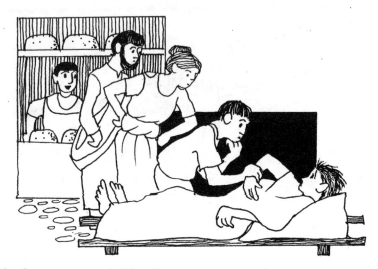

body scans and blood tests are used to locate the source of the trouble.

In Galen's time, diagnosis was not a science. In some places, an ailing person was carried out onto the street so passers-by could observe him and give their opinions on what was wrong. Not many diseases were known and danger signs might not be noticed until it was too late. Or even if the symptom was obvious, such as the pain of a ruptured appendix, nobody knew what or where an appendix was, so the patient died.

Even without the tools and tests a doctor has today, Galen was a brilliant diagnostician. He recognized familiar diseases — jaundice, diarrhea, leprosy, consumption and the "shaking disease," even though he didn't understand malaria. He decided how an illness should be treated, how long it might last and even if the patient was going to get well. He also knew if a patient was only imagining or pretending to be ill. Probably he treated make-believe illnesses with make-believe medicines — what we call placebos today.

His diagnoses were guided by the strong beliefs that he had held ever since his days at the Aesculapium and at Alexandria. He still thought that the pneuma and the three kinds of spirits in the body worked together.

Galen was determined to explain the place of every organ in the body and its purpose. He was sure that God had created a perfect design with each part of the body especially made to do a particular job.

There was the liver, the engine of life, controlling nutrition and changing food into blood. Galen was right in thinking that blood kept the life process going by nourishing the heart, lungs, brain and the other organs. He thought that each organ had the power to attract just the kind of nourishment it needed for itself.

There was the heart, directing the passions, regulating body temperature and somehow moving blood from organ to organ.

He still believed that the lungs breathed in pneuma and also cooled the heart. That was logical. The hot heart was surrounded by those cooling lungs.

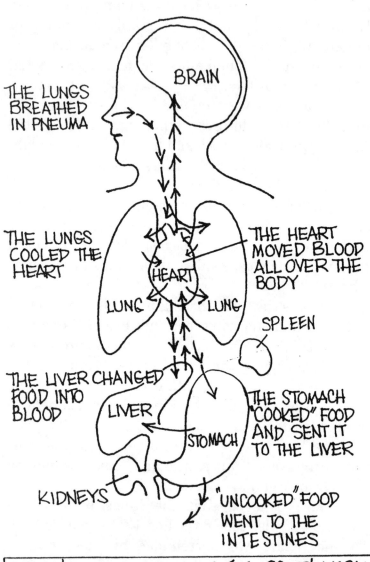

GALEN'S EXPLANATION OF THE ORGANS' WORK

He thought that blood went to the brain through tiny veins. Galen knew that it was important to nourish the brain, which controlled all movement and all sensations.

What about the stomach? It seemed to be a central storehouse, located in the middle of the body. Galen thought the stomach "cooked" the food people ate. He was right —we call that cooking, digestion. The stomach changed food into a thick liquid he called chyle (kile). He had seen sheets of muscles in the stomach walls of the animals he dissected and he thought that they did the stomach's work by squeezing. Nobody understood the role of chemicals in the body.

The stomach kept some chyle for its own needs and sent the rest through the veins to the liver. The "uncooked" food fell to the bottom of the stomach and went, as waste, to the intestines and the bowels to be gotten rid of.

Once Galen had described the organs and how they functioned, his next step was to figure out what part they played in disease. Galen absolutely believed in the four body fluids which were associated with the organs. He thought that the humors had everything to do with disease.

He believed that the humors must always be kept in balance. If they were out of balance — if there was too much or not enough of one of the humors — a person became ill.

Now we know that it is a balance of body chemicals — not humors — that keep people healthy. But Galen was on the right track.

Both biles and phlegm were visible mainly in disease, so he thought they were harmful humors. Too much blood might be harmful, but usually blood was a helpful humor.

Galen said that even if the imbalance seemed to affect the whole body — perhaps the patient had a high fever — the imbalance could be traced to a particular organ. Since Galen knew (or thought he knew) the connection between a humor and its organ, the illness could be located. Then the doctor, Galen or another, could make a diagnosis and prescribe a remedy to restore the balance.

To cure the imbalance the cure might be a change of diet. For example, he believed that a fever was caused by too much yellow bile (dry and hot), so he prescribed first, compresses of cold water, lots of cool liquids, and finally, thyme or mint tea.

The cure for coughing (too much phlegm) might be a change of scene — getting away from the city or the marshes, to the mountains. If that wasn't possible, lots of garlic juice and ginger. But Galen thought that coughing wasn't all bad; it helped the body get rid of yellow bile and phlegm.

Mashed garlic was also prescribed if the patient couldn't sleep.

Many cures might be simply a change of lifestyle
— eating less, getting to bed earlier and getting
more exercise.

Or the cure might be bleeding, purging, throwing
up, or doses of medicine. Galen disapproved of surgery, except to repair an injury.

What led Galen, and before him, Empedocles and
Hippocrates, to believe that the humors existed at
all? Well, some of those body fluids were obvious.

There was no problem in identifying blood, or
phlegm. And the humor they called yellow bile
seemed to appear when someone vomited, or as pus
from a sore.

But what about black bile? Maybe it was the
dark, dark stuff that showed up in infected wounds,
or was excreted when a patient was very ill. But

where did it come from? If every humor was connected to an organ, what was black bile's organ?

Tucked up against the stomach is a smallish, dark organ called the spleen. Galen called the spleen the organ of mystery.

Ever since Hippocrates, doctors had been wondering what the spleen did in the body. Some thought it controlled the emotions. Some thought it made a runner fast or slow. Some thought it made a person bad-tempered. We know now that the spleen is a kind of filter that helps resist infection.

Galen decided that the spleen stored black bile, which was the waste left over from the liver when, as he thought, it made blood. He thought the spleen helped the body to get rid of excess black bile.

Actually, black bile was imaginary. (So were the other humors, really, but at least they were visible liquids.) If the Greek theory of four of everything was true, there had to be a fourth humor, so black bile was made up to be that fourth.

Galen also believed in Hippocrates' idea that there were four basic temperaments, depending on which humor a person had the most of. As Galen got to know his patients, he connected their dispositions to their humors.

A cheerful and lively patient had an extra supply of blood. (We still say that nice, friendly people have a sanguine disposition. This word comes from the Latin word for blood.)

People who were calm and slow-moving had phlegm as their most important humor. (You might want to look up the word, "phlegmatic" in your dictionary.)

Some patients who were really energetic were also quick to get angry. People who had big tempers had a lot of yellow bile.

The patients who were depressed and gloomy had too much black bile. When they were ill, they were least likely to get well.

Galen used other ideas in diagnosing and treating his patients. He understood that sometimes the mind, not the body was in control. He said, "Medicine cures many illnesses, but has its limits. Matters which are not understood can cause illness."

Hippocrates, and Galen after him, did not believe in the popular idea that insanity came from the gods. They thought that mental disorders were real diseases that came from natural causes. Galen prescribed treatment programs such as quiet, soothing occupations, and drugs, such as hellebore, a purgative. In Rome, most disturbed people were taken care of by their families. So were ill people. Except for the Temples of Aesculapius, hospitals were only for soldiers.

In Galen's time and for thousands of years before and after, everyone — doctors, scientists, slaves, philosophers, craftsmen — everyone believed in astrology. People believed that the stars and the moon, the planets and the constellations, influenced everything that happened on earth. The month and the day, even the hour of your birth, decided your future.

Doctors — even Galen — consulted astrologers, who drew up charts that were supposed to show which heavenly bodies were affecting their patients and these charts were used to help diagnose an illness. We know now that those things do not influence people's personal lives.

Galen didn't believe in magic, but he liked to have his patients think he had a mysterious power in medicine, even though his cures were not magical at all. He wanted people to wonder at his powers, so he allowed them to have magic charms, if they believed in them.

One of Galen's books was called, *On Diagnosis From Dreams.* Galen believed that a patient's dreams were helpful in diagnosing an illness. He said dreams were visions-in-sleep.

Some dreams, he said, were nothing more than left-over impressions of what a person had been doing or thinking during the day. But others showed an imbalance in a patient's humors.

He said it was likely that in sleep the soul had retreated from the sensations and influences of the world around it and had gone deep into its body to understand what was wrong and to reveal, through a dream, what were the excesses and lacks in its humors.

Did a wrestler dream he was standing in a pool of blood? He had too much blood and needed bleeding.

Did a patient dream of smoke, mist and deep darkness? She was troubled by black bile.

And what about a dream of snow, ice and hail? Cold phlegm was the problem.

Galen paid attention to how dreams changed during the different stages of a disease. Of course dreams were only one of his ways of diagnosing and treating his patients. He was also a great believer in medicines.

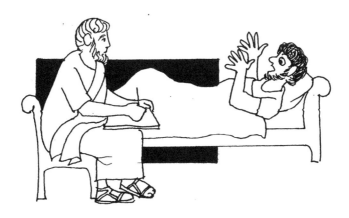

Galen's Pharmacy

Pharmacy is the art and science of preparing drugs. In medicine, a drug is a plant, animal, mineral or chemical substance that is given to prevent or cure illness.

A pharmacy is a place where medicines are prepared.

Galen was really interested in preparing and inventing medicines.

Today, a doctor calls the pharmacy and orders a prescription — pills, capsules, liquids, injections, powders, ointments. There are thousands of choices in many different kinds of doses. Galen couldn't order medicine for his patients. He had to make his own, so he had his own pharmacy.

The pharmacy stocked herbs, spices and many other plants, stored in glass bottles and clay jars, in linen sacks or hanging to dry from the ceiling. There were also minerals and different kinds of soil, dried or powdered animal parts and animal products, such as beeswax, honey and milk. Ships coming into Ostia from all over the ancient world brought the raw materials that were used to make medicines.

There were merchants in Rome whose only business was importing and selling drugs. Some were honest, but Galen felt that most were cheats, supplying ingredients that were of no value at all. Worthless mixtures were also sold by peddlars from all over the countryside around Rome.

Galen made long journeys himself to get ingredients he trusted. Ever since he had been a student he had observed and collected plants and he had a thorough knowledge of them. Whenever he traveled to a new place he went into the fields looking for new plants that might make medicines. And he talked with people in the countryside, asking how they were using plants that were unfamiliar to him, as cures.

He also ordered supplies from people he knew abroad — from Egypt, from the Greek Islands, from the province of Asia and even from caravaners who brought ingredients from the far east.

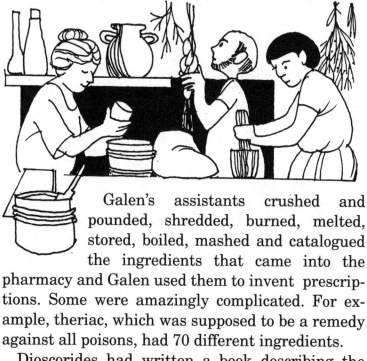

Galen's assistants crushed and pounded, shredded, burned, melted, stored, boiled, mashed and catalogued the ingredients that came into the pharmacy and Galen used them to invent prescriptions. Some were amazingly complicated. For example, theriac, which was supposed to be a remedy against all poisons, had 70 different ingredients.

Dioscorides had written a book describing the plants he used for medicine, but Galen was the first pharmacist to measure precise amounts of everything he used in preparing a remedy. He kept careful records of how each was made and the dose which had to be given. Then he noted the patient's reaction to each dose and changed the dose when necessary. He believed that the amount of the dose

determined whether it had a small or a strong effect on the patient. Too much could be harmful or even fatal.

Scribes wrote down every word Galen dictated as he worked. The words became thirty books on pharmacy. The books are called Galen's *Pharmacopoeia* (FAR-ma-ka-PEE-ah). A pharmacopoeia is a list of drugs accepted by most of the medical people who use them, along with the source of the drug, the way it is prepared and the standard dose. Galen's pharmacopoeia was a standard reference for more than 1,500 years.

Some of Galen's prescriptions had to be strong, smelly, ugly, and bad tasting. But when he could, he made them sweet, mildly perfumed and brightly colored, so patients wouldn't object to taking them.

Galen listed and described more than 700 plant ingredients he used in his prescriptions. Here are a few. How many are familiar to you?

Acacia and almond oil. Aloes for cuts, burns and bruises. Anise, barley and bay leaves. Bilberries (blueberries) for diarrhea. Cannabis, caraway and castor oil. Chamomile to treat malaria. Cinnamon, coriander, cloves, crocus, dates, dill. Garlic for preventing almost everything. Grapes, fern, figs, hellebore, hemlock, honey, honeysuckle, lavender, juniper, linseed, licorice and mandrake. Marshmallow (and mud) to heal inflammations. Marigold, mint, mold, moss, mustard, and myrrh. Oatmeal for making poultices and opium for pain. Onion, pepper, peppermint, poppy, pomegranate, rhubarb, rosemary, rue, scammony, sesame, spearmint, spikenard, squill, turpentine, vinegar and water. Some of these ingredients were worth much more than their weight in gold.

Do you know which of these are still used for their healing properties? A few familiar ones are aloes, garlic, figs and honey, mint, mold, moss, and, of course, water. How many more do you know?

Galen Serves the Emperors

For four years, Galen was at the center of life in
Rome. Then, suddenly, he decided to leave. He said
that he could no longer stand the meanness and
envy of the other doctors and their constant quarrels with him. But maybe that wasn't the real reason.

Ever since Marcus Aurelius and Lucius Verus had become emperors, Rome had been at war. The Roman legions were fighting in Britain, at the Rhine River, and the Danube. But the most serious fighting was in the east, in Armenia.

The battle went well, but soldiers returning to Rome brought plague with them. It wasn't doctorly, but Galen was terribly afraid of plague. Plague made even the greatest doctors helpless. No one knew where it came from or how it started. There was no medicine for it. If you got it, almost surely you died.

When we think of plague now, we think of bubonic (boo-BON-ic) or pneumonic (noo-MON-ic) plague, diseases of rodents, transmitted by rat fleas. The plague might start in crowded cities, where the fleas of infected rats jumped to people. But it might also start in the countryside if there were so many infected rodents that the fleas had nowhere else to jump except onto humans. And it was terribly infectious. Pneumonic plague spreads by simply breathing the infection in.

The plagues during Galen's time killed a third of the people in the empire. (Twelve hundred years later, the epidemic called the Black Death killed 25 million people — a quarter of the population of Europe.)

Actually, a plague might be any terrible epidemic. Before we knew what caused them, or how to prevent them, smallpox and measles were plagues. Influenza has been a plague, too. The plague that sent Galen away from Rome might have been smallpox.

Whatever his reason for leaving Rome was, Galen disposed of his household goods, set out on foot across the peninsula, sailed for Greece and traveled back to Pergamum.

Galen stayed in Pergamum until 168, when Marcus Aurelius summoned him back. The emperors were with their troops at Aquileia (a-KWEE-le-yuh) in northern Italy and they wanted their doctor with them.

ROMAN SOLDIERS BUILT THEIR OWN FORTS.

Germanic tribesmen, barbarians from the north who threatened to overwhelm the Empire, had crossed the Alps into Italy. To drive them back the emperors drafted every fit man — even gladiators and bandits — to fight with the Roman legions.

Galen was there at the front to serve the emperors, the generals and the royal court. He was not there to doctor the common soldiers.

Soldiers who were not too seriously wounded in a battle were cared for by their fellows, who cleaned their wounds, stitched them together and applied soothing ointments. These untrained doctors were ordinary soldiers who had showed a talent for wound dressing and simple surgery. They were called the medici.

If their wounds were not too serious, the troops went back into battle. Soldiers who were sick or badly wounded were taken to the hospital.

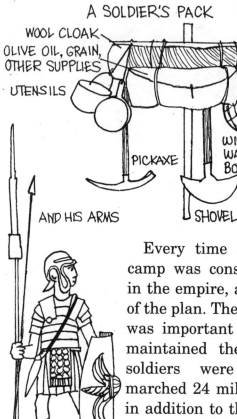

A SOLDIER'S PACK

WOOL CLOAK
OLIVE OIL, GRAIN, OTHER SUPPLIES
UTENSILS

WINE OR WATER BOTTLE

PICKAXE

AND HIS ARMS

SHOVEL

Every time a Roman military camp was constructed, anywhere in the empire, a hospital was part of the plan. The health of the army was important because the army maintained the empire. (Roman soldiers were amazing. They marched 24 miles a day, carrying, in addition to their equipment, all their own food. They carried olive oil, grain and the grindstones to grind the grain. At the end of each day's march they ground their own flour and baked their bread. With a little olive oil on it, that was their rations.)

When Roman engineers located new forts and camps for the army, they never built near marshes.

The engineers were informed that "In the neighborhood of marshes, certain minute creatures which cannot be seen float through the air and enter the body through the mouth and nose and cause serious diseases."

The Romans were also suspicious of fleas. Rue and mint repelled fleas, so soldiers wore rue and mint leaves and scattered them on their tent floors.

Camps were always built where there was plenty of clean, fresh water for bathing and for sanitation. When an old camp became contaminated, the legion moved on to a new camp.

Galen hated the camp and he hated the battlefield. He convinced Marcus to let him return to Rome to take care of Marcus' son, Commodus. The emperors themselves returned to Rome soon after, because plague had broken out in the camp.

MARCUS AURELIUS

Then they were off again. Before he left, Marcus gave the title, Caesar, to Commodus, although he was only fifteen. Galen stayed in Rome with Commodus, who was a difficult patient because he was somewhat mad.

LUCIUS VERUS

Both emperors spent the rest of their lives fighting. Lucius Verus, a good soldier who didn't care much about being an emperor, died on a march in 169.

Marcus Aurelius, a good emperor who didn't like being a soldier, died in camp at Vindobona, in 180. (Vindobona is now Vienna.)

COMMODUS
(HE LIKED TO DRESS
UP AS HERCULES.)

Commodus became a very bad emperor, but Galen continued to be his doctor. Commodus was murdered in 192, and Galen became doctor to the next emperor, Septimius Severus (SEP-ti-mus sev-AIR-us).

Very few people who knew him mourned Commodus. But Galen had a real and terrible loss that year. There was a fire in the Temple of Peace, where he had put many of his manuscripts for safe-keeping, and important parts of his work were burned. Still, many were saved and were widely circulated.

SEPTIMIUS SEVERUS

During the last twenty years of his life, Galen stayed in Rome. He made a few journeys to investigate scientific ideas that interested him. But mostly, he lived quietly and kept writing.

Altogether, his writings include essays, lectures and books — 78 books.

He wrote 30 books on pharmacy, the art and science of preparing medicine.

He wrote 17 books on physiology, which is about the functions of living organisms and their parts.

He wrote 16 books on therapeutics, the treatment of diseases.

He wrote 9 books on anatomy, the structure of animals and plants.

He wrote 6 books on pathology, the study of diseases.

His last writings seem to have been in the year 207, which is mysterious, too. Most biographies of Galen say that he died in 200, or 201. Others say he died in 210.

The Arabs were great collectors and translators of Galen's work and their biographies say that he died in 216 or 217, when he was 87 years old.

After Galen

During his lifetime Galen was so famous that medical students, doctors, scientists and anyone interested in science read everything he wrote. His writing was so popular that often forged papers appeared in book sellers' shops under his name. Forgers thought that anything supposed to be written by Galen would sell easily.

False Galen writings appeared for hundreds of years — first in Rome, then in the Middle East, then in Europe. But true or forged, there were so many writings that Galen's ideas were the greatest influence on medicine for centuries.

In the year 196, Emperor Septimius Severus, who was still fighting to keep the Roman Empire whole, captured Byzantium (by-ZAN-tee-um), an important city at the crossroads of Europe and Asia. Byzantium became Roman.

In 330 the Roman Emperor Constantine (CON-stan-teen) renamed the city Constantinople (con-stan-ta NO-ple) and made it the capital of the Roman empire. He made Christianity the official religion.

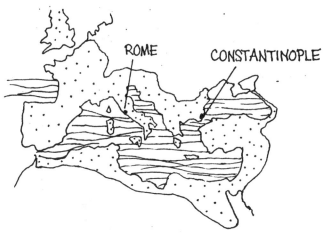

The power of the old Roman Empire was gone, but the Byzantine people still called themselves Romans. Their government was Roman and their language, culture and science were Greek. Galen's writings were taught in the medical schools and his ideas crowded out any other medical theories in the Byzantine world.

CONSTANTINE

In the world of the ninth century, the Arabs were the scientists, the mathematicians and the doctors. They translated Galen's manuscripts from Greek into Arabic and Aramaic, the everyday speech of the Middle East. Most medicine in the Arab world was Galen's medicine.

In Europe during that time people were not concerned with science or medicine. They were farmers and craftsmen, living in small towns, sometimes fighting for the lords who owned the towns. They lived simply. Learning was not part of their lives.

Greek knowledge and Greek language were almost forgotten. But scholars in monasteries preserved the writings of the ancient world. Then, in

AVICENNA, THE GREAT ARAB PHYSICIAN, REVERED THE WORK OF GALEN AND ARISTOTLE. HE LIVED IN THE 11th CENTURY.

the twelfth century, the classics of Greek science began to be translated into Latin—the works of Archimedes and Euclid, Hippocrates and Galen.

Now, in Europe, new universities were founded. They had medical schools, and Galen's ideas became the basic ideas of medical education. Even though a few doctors began to question some of those ideas, the Catholic Church supported Galen because they agreed with his belief in the perfect Creator, who had created a perfect human being.

Galen dominated the medicine of the Middle Ages. It was forbidden to argue with his writings.

IN THE MIDDLE AGES, GALEN WAS PICTURED LIKE THIS. HE WAS CALLED CLAUDIUS GALENUS.

The bridge to the modern world was the period called the Renaissance, which began in the fourteenth century. New kinds of art and literature appeared, and people began to question some of the old ideas about science. Questioning the old ideas meant questioning Galen, since he was the main source of so much medical practice.

One of the first to object to Galen's medicine was Paracelsus (par-ah-CELL-suss). His real name was Theophrastus Phillipus Aureolus Bombastus von Hohenheim! Paracelsus was the name he gave himself.

PARACELSUS

Paracelsus was the most original medical thinker since Galen. He introduced the idea of chemistry into medicine and said that chemical principles, not humors, underlie all nature. He argued that medicine should be based on chemicals, not botanicals. His ideas really were the beginning of biochemistry and molecular medicine.

In 1493 (Columbus had just returned from the new world) Paracelsus was born in the Swiss town of Basel (BA-zel). His father was a doctor and his mother was a nurse.

Paracelsus studied medicine, first with his father, and then in Italy, where he was expelled from his university for saying that doctors should abandon the outdated ideas of Hippocrates and Galen. He made fun of the four humors, which were still accepted by most doctors, and publicly burned Galen's books, saying they should never be taught.

Later, as an established doctor in Basel, Paracelsus became a popular lecturer, as Galen had been.

Paracelsus was a believer in alchemy, a "science" which would later become the real science of chemistry. (Alchemy is as "wrong" to us as the four humors were to him.) The main goal of alchemy was to change base metals, such as tin or iron, into gold. Paracelsus said that alchemists should have a new ambition — not to change minerals and metals into gold, but to change them into medicines.

Paracelsus scoffed at the traditional science of Galen's time, saying that it began with explanations, then tried to fit observations into them. He

said that true science should be open-minded, always questioning and looking for new explanations. So he wasn't really fair to Galen who was always observing and searching for new knowledge.

The next important objector to Galen's medicine was Andreas Vesalius (An-DREY-us Vis-AY-le-us),

ANDREAS VESALIUS

who was born in Brussels, in 1514. He was the son of the imperial court apothecary at Brussels, which was part of the Holy Roman Empire. (Today, Brussels is in Belgium.) Vesalius, at the age of 27, provided the first accurate description of the human body.

Vesalius was always fascinated by anatomy.Even as a boy, he dissected dead dogs, cats and mice to observe how they were made, inside.

Vesalius studied at the University of Paris, under a professor who was a champion of Galen. But, when Vesalius began to compare Galen's anatomy with what he had learned himself about the animals he dissected, he realized that Galen was not describing the anatomy of humans, but the anatomy of monkeys, pigs and goats. Galen had never dissected a human body!

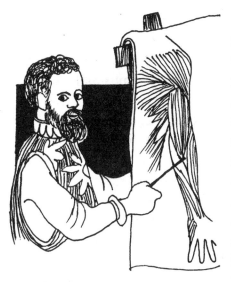

Vesalius searched for human bones in the Paris cemeteries, took them home and studied them carefully. Once, he even stole a body from the gallows because he wanted a skull of his own to study. It was legal, now, to dissect human bodies for teaching, learning and studying anatomy, so he was also able to dissect the bodies of criminals who had been executed.

Vesalius continued his studies at the University of Padua, in Italy, where he became a professor of anatomy and surgery when he was 23 years old.

His lectures were popular. Instead of teaching from a high desk overlooking the audience while a barber-surgeon worked on the body, Vesalius did his own dissections. He also made big charts showing and labeling the body parts. Anatomical drawings were something new. Vesalius published the charts, some with drawings by famous illustrators, some with his own drawings.

More and more, he understood why Galen had made mistakes. The anatomy of an ape or another animal was different from the anatomy of a human. So Vesalius decided to write and publish his own books on anatomy.

When the writing was finished, he traveled to Venice to work with a well-known illustrator. When the drawings for the books were finally done, the wooden blocks with the illustrations engraved on them were sent over the Alps on mule back.

Vesalius' books were called *De Fabrica*. (In English they are called "Structure of the Human Body.") They were published in Basel, Switzerland, in 1543, the same year that Copernicus put forth a new idea of the universe. *De Fabrica* was the first accurate description of the human body. Now anatomy had a language of its own.

When he presented his books to Charles V, the Holy Roman Emperor, Charles made Vesalius physician to the royal court.

WILLIAM HARVEY

The next great challenger to Galen's ideas was William Harvey, who was born in England in 1578.

Vesalius had corrected Galen's anatomy. Harvey took on Galen's theories about the function of the heart, and how blood moved to other organs.

Harvey entered Cambridge University at 17, graduated at 19, decided to be a doctor, and went to the famous medical school in Padua, Italy, to study.

Fabricus (FAB-ri-cus), Harvey's teacher at Padua, had made an interesting discovery years before when he noticed that the veins in human arms and legs contained tiny valves that allowed blood to flow in one direction only.

Harvey studied anatomy at Padua for five years. When he was 24 he returned to England and settled in London. Shakespeare and Ben Jonson were there at the same time, hard at work writing plays.

Harvey became a popular physician in London. His patients included Francis Bacon, the famous philosopher who was also the Lord Chancellor of England and one after another, the kings James I and Charles I. But Harvey's real interest was in studying the motions of the heart and the blood. He was curious about the pulse. Did it indicate the movement of blood?

Most doctors were still studying Galen's ideas — that blood was carried in blood vessels by some mysterious motion, passing through pores in the right side of the heart to the left side and going from there into the lungs. They were still teaching that air flowed from the lungs into the heart, keeping blood cool and supplying it with pneuma.

Harvey dissected different kinds of animals. He even saw and felt a beating heart. He studied the problem for years. In 1628 he published a small book — 67 pages — called, *On the Motion of Heart and of Blood in Animals.*

Harvey said that the heart was not a furnace. The heart was a pump. When the heart contracted, it forced blood out and when the heart relaxed, blood flowed in again.

He wrote that blood flowed in a continuous stream, always in one direction, through all parts of the body, over and over, from the heart back to the heart. He said that valves in the great arteries coming out of the heart permitted the blood to flow only away from the heart. And that valves in the veins allowed blood to pass only one way, to the heart.

Harvey said that the same blood is always pumped by the heart into the arteries and that same blood is always coming back through the veins. It circulates.

Harvey's book proved that almost everything that had been taught before about the heart and the blood was mistaken.

His book made him famous all over Europe, but there were still people who hated to throw out Galen's ideas which had been so important for so many centuries.

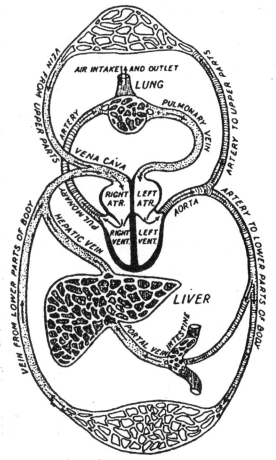

HARVEY'S THEORY OF BLOOD CIRCULATION

ARTERIES CARRIED BLOOD FROM THE HEART
TO ALL PARTS OF THE BODY.
VEINS CARRIED BLOOD FROM ALL PARTS
OF THE BODY BACK TO THE HEART.

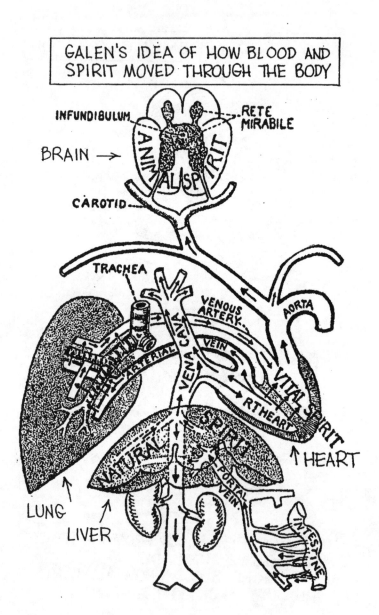

GALEN'S IDEA OF HOW BLOOD AND SPIRIT MOVED THROUGH THE BODY

William Harvey's work was the real bridge to modern medicine, as Galen's work had been the bridge from ancient medicine.

Galen's teachings and the hundreds of books and articles he wrote shaped medical practice for almost 1,500 years — through ancient times, through the middle ages and into the Renaissance. In a time when observation and experiment were almost the only tools a doctor had to move medicine along, his theories were something to build on.

Because Galen argued that illnesses (which he called an imbalance of humors) could be located in specific organs, doctors could make more accurate diagnoses and prescribe remedies to restore the body's balance.

Galen was careful and he was logical. His records organized medical knowledge in anatomy, physiology and pharmacy, and he was generous in sharing his knowledge and opinions. Some were right, some were wrong, but they were available to his profession.

Scientists start with ideas. Then they — or the scientists who follow — have to prove or disprove those ideas as new facts and new technologies emerge.

Galen was a genius. His ideas were a basis for the medical theories of later physicians. They were important steps along the way to new understandings of science and medicine.

For More Information on Galen

These books can be found in libraries:

The Great Doctors, by Henry Siegerist, Doubleday, Garden City

A Short History of Medicine, by Charles E. Singer and Ashworth Underwood, Oxford University Press, New York

The Mysteries Within, by Sherwin B. Nuland, Simon & Schuster, New York, 2000

The Great Men of Science, by Grove Wilson, Garden City Publishing

Great Books of the Western World, Vol. 10, Hippocrates and Galen, Encyclopedia Britannica

Index

INDEX

skeleton, 56, 57
skull, 57, 117
spinal chord, 80
spleen, 92
stomach, 5, 88-89, 92
teeth, 57
tendons, 68
throat, 57
tongue, 57
veins and arteries, 5, 35, 58-
60, 80, 89, 119, 120-121
vertebrae, 56, 80
vocal chords, 80

PEOPLE
Aesculapius, Greek god of
medicine, 25-29, 93
Temple of, see Pergamum
Alexander the Great, 16
Archimedes, 21, 113
Aristotle, 22, 32, 35, 58
Asclepiades, 78
Charles V, 118
Commodus, 83, 107
Constantine, 111
Copernicus, 118
Dioscorides, 46, 98
De Materia Medica, 46
Empedocles, 32, 39, 91
Erastistratus, 35
Euclid, 20-21, 113
The Elements, 21
Eudemus, philosophy
teacher of Galen, 72, 78
Fabricus, 119

Flavius Boethius, 79
Galileo, 21
Hadrian, 2
Harvey, William, 118-123
*On the Motion of Heart
and of Blood in Animals*,
120
Heraclides, father of
Hippocrates, 37
Herodotus, 22
Hippocrates, 36, 37-42, 91-
92, 93, 115
Hirophilus, 35
Lucius Verus, 83, 103,
107-108
Marc Antony and Cleopatra,
56
Marcus Aurelius, 83, 103,m
104, 107, 108
Minos, 50
Minotaur, 50
Nero, 46
Nicon, father of Galen, 10,
12-15, 18, 24, 28, 43, 46,
72
Paracelsus, 114-116
Pelops, 43, 46, 47
Plato, 22
Ptolemy, King, 16, 35
Ptolemy, astronomer and
geographer, 54-55
Almagest, 55
Geographia, 55
Refinus, medical teacher of
Galen, 29

INDEX

Satyrus, medical teacher of
   Galen, 29
Septimus Severus, 108, 111
Vesalius, 116-118
   De Fabrica, 118

PLACES
   Alexandria, 16, 35, 49, 50,
     51, 52-56, 61, 73, 87
     library of, 16, 35, 53, 55
     medical school, 35
     The Museum, 35, 36, 49,
     51, 52-57
     Pharos, 50
     school of mathematics,
     20
   Aquileia, 104
   Athens, 14, 22
   Basel, 114, 115, 118
   Brussels, 116
   Byzantium
     (Constantinople), 111
   Cambridge, University of,
     119
   Corinth, 47-49
   Cos, school of medicine, 37
   Crete, 49-50
   Lesbos, 48
   London, 119
   Ostia, 71-2, 97
   Padua, University of, 117,
     119
   Pergamum (Bergama), 2, 3,
     9-18, 25, 32, 42, 43, 44,

     47, 61, 62-63, 70, 71, 73,
     76, 104
   Aesculapium, 25, 26, 28,
     29, 43, 62, 67, 87, 93
     library of, 16, 17, 32, 56
     Ludi (school for
     gladiators), 63
   Rome, 2, 64, 70, 71-78, 83,
     97, 102-104, 108, 110
     Baths, 76, Circus
     Maximus, 73,
     Colosseum, 64, 73,
     Forum, 73, Sacred Way,
     73, Temple of Peace, 108
   Sicily, 32
   Smyrna, 43, 44, 45, 46, 47,
     48, 49
   Venice, 118
   Vindobona (Vienna) 108

PLANTS see MEDICINES

STUDIES
   alchemy, 115
   arithmetic, 20
   astrology, defined 40, 78, 94
   astronomy, 21, 35, 55
   botany, defined 46, 47, 50
   chemistry, 114
   geography, 55
   geometry, 20, 24
   history, 22
   mathematics, 20, 21, 22, 35
   philosophy, 23, 24, 46, 53
   science, 7, 21, 23, 113-114

INDEX

131

About the Author

JEANNE BENDICK, a graduate of Parsons School of Design, is the author and illustrator of many books, primarily in the field of science. Her work has always been distinguished by her remarkable ability to express complex concepts in simple language, and to make difficult subjects interesting and comprehensible to the general reader. Among her many books, the following are of interest, as related to the history of science or medicine: *Archimedes and the Door of Science, Along Came Galileo, Egyptian Tombs*, and *Super People*.